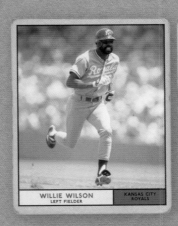
WILLIE WILSON
LEFT FIELDER
KANSAS CITY
ROYALS

DARRELL PORTER
CATCHER
KANSAS CITY
ROYALS

THE STORY OF THE KANSAS CITY ROYALS

Published by Creative Education
P.O. Box 227, Mankato, Minnesota 56002
Creative Education is an imprint of The Creative Company
www.thecreativecompany.us

Design and production by Blue Design
Art direction by Rita Marshall
Printed by Corporate Graphics in the United States of America

Photographs by Corbis (Bettmann), Getty Images (Bernstein Associates, Peter Brouillet, Bruce Bennett Studios, Kevin C. Cox, Richard Cummins, Mark Cunningham/MLB Photos, Jonathan Daniel, Diamond Images, Focus on Sport, Otto Greule Jr, Richard Mackson/Sports Illustrated, National Baseball Hall of Fame Library/MLB Photos, G. Newman Lowrance, Rich Pilling/MLB Photos, Jamie Squire, Jamie Squire/ Allsport, Rick Stewart, Josh Umphrey, Ron Vesely/MLB Photos, John Williamson/MLB Photos)

Library of Congress Cataloging-in-Publication Data

LeBoutillier, Nate.
The story of the Kansas City Royals / by Nate LeBoutillier.
p. cm. — (Baseball: the great American game)
Includes index.
Summary: The history of the Kansas City Royals professional baseball team from its inaugural 1969 season to today, spotlighting the team's greatest players and most memorable moments.
ISBN 978-1-60818-043-1
1. Kansas City Royals (Baseball team)—History—Juvenile literature. I. Title. II. Series.

GV875.K3L43 2011
796.357'6409778411—dc22   2010024400

CPSIA: 110310 PO1381

First Edition
9 8 7 6 5 4 3 2 1

Page 3: Outfielder David DeJesus
Page 4: Infielder Alberto Callaspo

BASEBALL: THE GREAT AMERICAN GAME

THE STORY OF THE KANSAS CITY ROYALS

Nate LeBoutillier

CREATIVE EDUCATION

CONTENTS

CHAPTERS

Royal Lineage 6

Tasting Success 15

A Crowning Achievement 25

The Drought Begins 33

New Nobles 37

AROUND THE HORN

Original Royalty 12

Pine Tar Problem 20

The Call 24

Season of Sadness 31

Kansas City's Castle 38

A Royal Mess 43

ALL-TIME ROYALS

P — Bret Saberhagen 8

C — Darrell Porter 13

1B — Mike Sweeney 14

2B — Frank White 18

3B — George Brett 23

SS — Freddie Patek 28

LF — Willie Wilson 30

CF — Amos Otis 35

RF — Bo Jackson 39

M — Dick Howser 40

Index 48

ROYAL LINEAGE

Located at the convergence of the Missouri and Kansas rivers and near the geographic center of the 48 contiguous United States is Kansas City, Missouri. Officially settled just prior to the Civil War, Kansas City, in its formative years, was deeply embroiled in the slavery issue that divided the country, as it sat along the line between North and South. In the years that followed the Civil War and the abolition of slavery, Kansas City's population boomed, and the city became one of the largest in the American heartland.

Kansas City first hosted a professional baseball team in 1920, when the Kansas City Monarchs, a charter member of the Negro Leagues, began play. In 1955, the city welcomed the Athletics, an American League (AL) team that had started out in 1901 in Philadelphia, Pennsylvania. Unfortunately, the Kansas City Athletics had very little success, and in 1967, after a mere 13 seasons, franchise owners decided to relocate to Oakland, California. The "A's" moved, but big-league baseball did not. In 1969, Major League Baseball granted a new

Although Kansas City was once home to professional basketball and hockey franchises, it today hosts only football's Chiefs and baseball's Royals.

PITCHER · BRET SABERHAGEN

When Bret Saberhagen joined the Royals' starting rotation in 1984, he was just 20 years old. But despite his youth, he showed remarkable poise and control, which would become hallmarks of his 16-year major-league career. He won 10 games that first season and doubled that total in 1985, when he became the youngest player ever to win the Cy Young Award and was named series Most Valuable Player (MVP) in the Royals' World Series victory over the St. Louis Cardinals. Saberhagen played for eight years with the Royals and was inducted into the team's Hall of Fame in 2005.

BRET SABERHAGEN
PITCHER

KANSAS CITY
ROYALS

STATS

Royals seasons: 1984–91

Height: 6-foot-1

Weight: 180

- **3-time All-Star**

- **167 career wins**

- **2-time Cy Young Award winner**

- **1,715 career strikeouts**

AL team to Kansas Citians, and the Royals set up shop in the city's Municipal Stadium.

Three other teams—the Milwaukee Brewers, San Diego Padres, and Montreal Expos—were also incorporated into the majors in 1969, but the Royals, with a 69–93 record, finished with the best mark of the four. One of the reasons the Royals were so successful right off the bat was rookie left fielder Lou Piniella. Standing six feet tall, with a barrel chest and skinny legs, Piniella wasn't the fastest player in the game, but he was smart, and his .282 batting average with 11 home runs and 68 runs batted in (RBI) was good enough to earn him AL Rookie of the Year honors. Dick Drago was the club's top performer on the mound, going 11–13 in the Royals' inaugural season and throwing two complete-game shutouts.

When the Royals got off to a dismal start in 1970, the club made a change in the dugout, hiring legendary pitcher Bob Lemon to take over as manager. In 1971, Lemon guided the Royals to their first winning season in just their third year of existence, at the time the quickest any expansion team had ever turned in a winning record. Unfortunately, Kansas City's 85–76 mark ranked a distant second to the AL Western

Division champions, Kansas City's former team, the Athletics.

Although the Royals took a step backward in 1972, they started 1973 with a winning attitude. They had just moved out of rickety Municipal Stadium and into beautiful Royals Stadium, their new, state-of-the-art home. With fan favorite Cookie Rojas at second, speedy Freddie Patek at shortstop, and slick-fielding Amos Otis in center field, the team looked ready to take off. On August 2, the team's outlook brightened further as Kansas City brought up a 20-year-old third baseman who would exceed even the wildest expectations of Royals management and fans—George Brett.

By the time Brett joined the team, the Royals were 62–48 and on their way to a second-place finish. Over the next few years, Brett helped lead the Royals' charge to the very top of the division. In 1976, he won his first AL batting crown with a .333 average, and the team captured its first division title with 90 wins before falling to the New York Yankees in the AL Championship Series (ALCS), losing three games to two. In 1977, the Royals cruised to a second straight division title with a franchise-best 102–60 record, but the Yankees foiled them in the ALCS once again.

GEORGE BRETT

AMOS OTIS

Amos Otis's minor-league and early big-league seasons (with the Boston Red Sox and New York Mets) were bumpy, as he was shifted around at the infield positions. His career took off after he arrived in Kansas City and settled in at center field.

SATCHEL PAIGE

ORIGINAL ROYALTY

Long before the Kansas City Royals played their first game, another royal family called the city home: the Kansas City Monarchs, a charter member of the Negro National League (NNL) in 1920. The Monarchs, whose golden crown logo was quite similar to that of the modern Royals, played a total of 37 seasons in the Negro Leagues, making it the longest-running franchise in league history. And in that long history, the team sent more players (including such legends as second baseman Jackie Robinson, pitcher Satchel Paige, and first baseman Ernie Banks) into major league baseball than any other Negro League team. The

Monarchs, whose 13 league championships earned them comparisons to the New York Yankees, played in the NNL until it disbanded in 1930; after "barnstorming" (touring the country as an independent team without a league affiliation) for most of the 1930s, the Monarchs became a charter member of the Negro American League (NAL) in 1937. The NAL dissolved in 1962, but the Monarchs continued playing for three more years before officially disbanding. The team's long history, and the history of the Negro Leagues in America, is today celebrated at the Negro Leagues Baseball Museum, which is fittingly located in Kansas City.

CATCHER · DARRELL PORTER

Darrell Porter's 4 seasons with the Royals were the best of his 17-year big-league career. The strong-armed catcher became a fan favorite for his intensity on the field. He routinely recorded one of the highest percentages of base runners thrown out and, in 1979, became just the second catcher in history to tally 100 walks, runs, and RBI in a season. He may be best known, however, as one of the first professional athletes to publicly admit to a substance abuse problem, checking himself into a rehabilitation center in 1980. Sadly, although he worked hard to overcome his addiction, it claimed his life in 2002.

DARRELL PORTER
CATCHER

KANSAS CITY
ROYALS

STATS

Royals seasons: 1977–80

Height: 6 feet

Weight: 193

- 4-time All-Star

- 188 career HR

- 1,369 career hits

- 826 career RBI

FIRST BASEMAN · MIKE SWEENEY

Everything changed when Mike Sweeney switched from catcher to first base in 1999. He struggled defensively at first (committing 12 errors in just 74 games) but his power hitting took off. After hitting 8 home runs in 1998, he suddenly slugged 22 balls out of the park and led the team with a .322 average. He followed that up with a career-best year in 2000, hitting 29 homers, driving in 144 runs, and making the first of 5 All-Star Game appearances. Often named in trade talks, Sweeney, after playing 13 seasons in Kansas City, was sent to Oakland prior to the 2008 season.

STATS

Royals seasons: 1995–2007

Height: 6-foot-3

Weight: 220

- **5-time All-Star**

- **.297 career BA**

- **909 career RBI**

- **6 seasons of 20-plus HR**

MIKE SWEENEY
FIRST BASEMAN

KANSAS CITY
ROYALS

The same story played out in 1978. The Royals had a remarkable regular season, winning the AL West for the third consecutive year. But the team could muster only one playoff win in yet another Yankees confrontation, a 10–4 victory in Game 2 of the ALCS. Even so, the team put a positive spin on the experience. "We didn't look at losing to the Yankees as a big defeat," star second baseman Frank White later said. "We looked at it as a steppingstone to the future."

TASTING SUCCESS

Brett led the league with 212 hits in 1979, and left fielder Willie Wilson paced all big-leaguers with 83 stolen bases, but Kansas City finished behind the California Angels in the AL West, out of the playoffs for the first time in four years. Royals manager Whitey Herzog was then fired and replaced by Jim Frey.

Frey's goal in his first season as skipper was to get back to the postseason and exact revenge on the team that had continually stymied the Royals—the Yankees. His players were happy to help: Wilson led the league in hits (230), runs scored (133), and triples (15), while reliever Dan Quisenberry used his distinctive submarine delivery to tally an AL-high 33 saves. But the most impressive performance in 1980 was that of AL Most Valuable Player (MVP) George Brett, whose .390 batting average easily topped the league and, for a time, looked like it might top .400—a feat that had not been accomplished since Boston Red Sox great Ted Williams had done it in 1941. "I know I've captured a lot of media attention this past season," Brett said, "but the Royals have a team built on teamwork, not on individuals."

The Royals finished the 1980 season 97–65 and, as expected, found themselves facing the Yankees in the ALCS. Fine pitching earned Kansas City wins in the first two games. In Game 3, the Yankees were clinging to a 2–1 lead in the top of the seventh inning. But then Brett blasted a three-run homer off a Goose Gossage pitch deep into the night—all the way to the third tier of the outfield stands. "I remember the crack of the bat," said Gossage. "The noise of the bat, it was like nothing I had ever heard before. I will never forget that crack. And then the silence."

DAN QUISENBERRY

SECOND BASEMAN · FRANK WHITE

Frank White had the tall task of replacing the immensely popular Cookie Rojas at second base in 1973. But by the time his 18-year tenure with Kansas City had ended, White had also earned the love and respect of the fans. He was an exceptional fielder who played 62 straight errorless games in 1977 and collected 8 Gold Glove awards for his defense.

Although he was never known as a power hitter, he twice hit 22 home runs and drove in 886 runs in his career. After retiring in 1990, White stayed with the organization as a coach and minor-league manager.

FRANK WHITE
SECOND BASEMAN

KANSAS CITY ROYALS

STATS

Royals seasons: 1973–90

Height: 5-foot-11

Weight: 170

- **2-time AL leader in fewest errors by a second baseman**

- **5-time All-Star**

- **Uniform number (20) retired by Royals**

- **Royals Hall of Fame inductee (1995)**

That majestic home run sent the jubilant Royals to the World Series, where they met the Philadelphia Phillies. Unfortunately, it was the Royals' fans who were ultimately silenced this time. Kansas City lost the first two games in Philadelphia before heading home. A solo home run by Brett in the first inning of Game 3 sparked the team to a 4–3 victory, and Royals first baseman Willie Aikens hit two long balls to help win Game 4. But those would be the only wins for Kansas City; Philadelphia won Games 5 and 6 to take home the trophy.

The Royals sputtered the following season, losing 30 of their first 50 games before the season was halted by a players' strike. Frey was fired shortly after the strike ended. Under his replacement, Dick Howser, the Royals won 20 of their last 33 games. Owning the best record within the division after the strike, Kansas City then faced Oakland, which had "won" the division before the strike, in an AL Division Series (ALDS). Kansas City never got on track, and Oakland swept the series in three games.

Although Wilson led the league with a .332 batting average, outfielder Hal McRae topped the AL with 133 RBI, and Quisenberry

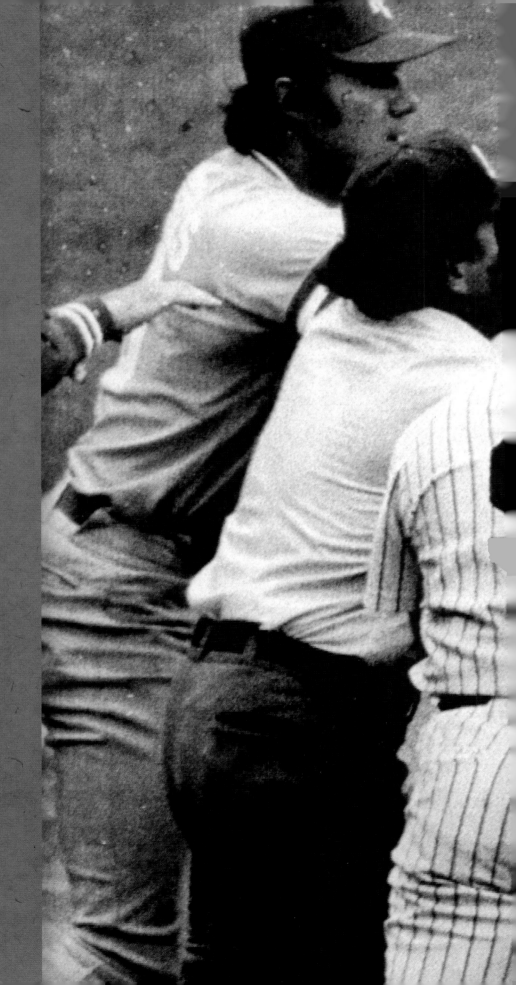

PINE TAR PROBLEM

The Royals trailed the New York Yankees, 4–3, with two outs in the top of the ninth on July 24, 1983, at Yankee Stadium. Yankees ace Goose Gossage was on the mound, and Kansas City star George Brett was at the plate—a classic matchup of longtime rivals. Brett slammed a two-run homer into the stands, scoring the go-ahead run as he crossed home plate. But just after Brett disappeared into the dugout, Yankees manager Billy Martin stepped out of his and approached home plate umpire Tim McClelland. Moments later, McClelland requested Brett's bat. He and the rest of the umpiring crew conferred, then abruptly called Brett out: the pine tar (a substance used to improve grip) on the handle of his bat, they said, exceeded the 18-inch limit. A furious Brett stormed out of the dugout, his eyes bulging. His teammates had to physically restrain the normally mild-mannered player, who was immediately ejected. A later appeal to AL president Lee MacPhail reversed the call on the grounds that "games should be won and lost on the playing field, not through technicalities of the rules." The two teams were forced to finish the game again on August 18 in New York; this time, the Royals won without any dispute, 5–4.

notched 35 saves, 1982 also ended in disappointment for the Royals, who went 90–72 but missed the postseason. The following year looked promising until four Royals players were charged with attempting to purchase cocaine. After the incident, the team, which had been on pace for a winning year, finished 20 games out of first with a 79–83 record.

Kansas City's 1984 season started with several new names on the roster, including Bret Saberhagen, a 20-year-old pitcher who had notched 18 wins in the Royals' minor-league system the previous year. Although the young phenom hadn't been selected until the 19th round of the 1982 draft, his pinpoint control and surprising maturity quickly earned him a spot in the Royals' rotation. As a rookie, he won 10 games and helped lead Kansas City back to a division title with an 84–78 record. Although the Detroit Tigers powered past the Royals in the playoffs, Saberhagen's heroics on the mound reenergized the Kansas City faithful.

THIRD BASEMAN · GEORGE BRETT

As a 20-year-old rookie in 1973, George Brett thought he knew what a Hall-of-Famer looked like: Carl Yastrzemski. So Kansas City's young third baseman modeled his batting stance after the Boston Red Sox star outfielder's. Twenty-one years later, when Brett retired with a .305 lifetime batting average, it was *his* posture that younger players were imitating. Brett, who spent his entire career with the Royals and came to epitomize the franchise, was the first player in major-league history to end his playing days with more than 3,000 hits, 300 home runs, 600 doubles, 100 triples, 1,500 RBI, and 200 stolen bases.

GEORGE BRETT
THIRD BASEMAN

KANSAS CITY
ROYALS

STATS

Royals seasons: 1973–93

Height: 6 feet

Weight: 190

- **13-time All-Star**

- **3,154 career hits**

- **317 career HR**

- **Baseball Hall of Fame inductee (1999)**

THE CALL

In Game 6 of the "I-70 Series," the St. Louis Cardinals led 1–0 and needed to get just three more outs to dispatch the Royals and take home the 1985 World Series crown. Pinch hitter Jorge Orta led off for the Royals in their last-gasp ninth inning. He nubbed a grounder left of first base that Cardinals first baseman Jack Clark fielded and scooped to pitcher Todd Worrell, who covered the bag as Orta hustled down the line. In a bang-bang play, Orta was called safe by umpire Don Denkinger, though replays showed that Worrell clearly touched the bag first. "The Call"—as elated Royals fans and angry Cardinals fans forever after referred to it—stood, though, and the play sparked a Kansas City rally that netted two runs, and the Royals won Game 6. In Game 7, Denkinger was the home plate umpire. After the Royals had taken a 10–0 lead by the fifth inning, Denkinger ejected St. Louis manager Whitey Herzog and pitcher Joaquín Andújar from the game for arguing balls and strikes. The Royals won the game, 11–0, to claim the championship. Although Denkinger received death threats following The Call, he continued to umpire major-league games until his retirement in 1998.

A CROWNING ACHIEVEMENT

**M**any Royals players put together outstanding individual seasons in 1985. But the biggest surprise was Saberhagen, who, at the tender age of 21, won 20 games and became the youngest player ever to win the coveted Cy Young Award as the league's best pitcher. His teammates were as impressed as the rest of the league.

"I was always amazed not only by the velocity of his fastball but by the command of his fastball," Royals pitcher Mark Gubicza said. Saberhagen's precision helped put the 91–71 Royals back in the postseason, where they met the Toronto Blue Jays in the first best-of-seven ALCS. Kansas City started slow but finished strong, coming back from a three-games-to-one deficit to win the series and gain entrance to the World Series.

BRET SABERHAGEN

The 1985 World Series was nicknamed the "I-70 Series," after the interstate linking Kansas City to its opponent, the St. Louis Cardinals. Although the series started on the Kansas City side of Missouri, the Royals fell behind three games to two and were on the brink of elimination by the time the series returned to Kansas City for Game 6. The Cardinals had a 1–0 lead in the ninth and were ready to celebrate when the Royals got a much-needed break: leadoff hitter Jorge Orta was called safe on a close play at first, although replays showed he was out. The controversial call infuriated the St. Louis dugout and enabled a two-run, game-winning rally for the Royals that pushed the series to a seventh game. And that gave Saberhagen the opportunity to win the series for Kansas City. Before a crowd of more than 41,000, he pitched a masterful shutout that finally ended 11–0. The young pitcher, whose first child had been born the night before, was then named series MVP. "What more can I ask for?" Saberhagen said. "It's like the world's at my feet."

That euphoric feeling didn't last long. The next season was a disappointment for the Royals, whose 76–86 record (the team's first losing mark in four years) told only part of the story. Manager Dick Howser was diagnosed with a cancerous brain tumor just after the midseason All-Star break. Although he tried to come back after

1985 WORLD SERIES

SHORTSTOP · FREDDIE PATEK

At 5-foot-5, Freddie Patek was the smallest major-league player of his time. But the talented shortstop, whose stature earned him the nickname "The Flea," never let height get in the way of stopping a sharply hit ball or firing accurate throws across the field. He had remarkable range, a strong arm, and catlike reflexes that made him adept at turning double plays in the field; he executed more than 1,000 in his career. Although not a power hitter, Patek had speed on his side; he led the AL with 11 triples in 1971 and 53 stolen bases in 1977.

STATS

Royals seasons: 1971–79

Height: 5-foot-5

Weight: 148

- 3-time All-Star
- 385 career stolen bases
- 490 career RBI
- Hit for the cycle (a single, double, triple, and HR in the same game) on July 9, 1971

FREDDIE PATEK
SHORTSTOP

KANSAS CITY
ROYALS

surgery in 1987, by March his illness had forced him to resign. The Royals managed to win 83 games in 1987, but they lost their leader when Howser died in the middle of the season.

The team's heartache was only slightly tempered by the emergence of several talented young players—most notably Bo Jackson, a Heisman Trophy winner (as college football's best player) who initially chose to play pro baseball rather than football after college. In 1987, the muscle-bound outfielder demonstrated his immense potential by hitting 22 home runs. He also announced that he was signing a contract with the Los Angeles Raiders to play professional football "as a hobby." His two-sport status didn't seem to affect his ability to perform, however. In 1988, he slugged 25 home runs and helped Kansas City finish third in the AL West. When Jackson led the team with 32 long balls in 1989, Kansas City improved to second place. Then a hip injury—suffered while playing football—hampered Jackson's ability, and the Royals plummeted to 75–86 the following year.

When Jackson's career with the Royals ended after the 1990 season, the Royals were desperate for new talent. Promising

LEFT FIELDER · WILLIE WILSON

Willie Wilson is widely considered the fastest Royals player ever—perhaps the fastest in the majors as well. Of his 802 base-stealing attempts, he slid in safely 668 times, including a league-leading 83 times in 1979. But speed wasn't the talented outfielder's only gift; Wilson picked up a Gold Glove award in 1980, won an AL batting title with a .332 average in 1982, and played in two All-Star Games. Although his reputation was tarnished by drug charges in 1983, Wilson's 15 years with the Royals eventually earned him a spot in the team Hall of Fame.

STATS

Royals seasons: 1976–90

Height: 6-foot-3

Weight: 195

- 2-time All-Star

- .285 career BA

- 147 career triples

- Royals Hall of Fame inductee (2000)

WILLIE WILSON
LEFT FIELDER

KANSAS CITY
ROYALS

SEASON OF SADNESS

Tears rolled down from behind Dick Howser's sunglasses as he gathered his players for a team meeting at the end of February 1987. "I can't do it," he told them. After two surgeries to remove a tumor found in his brain the previous year, Howser had tried valiantly to return to the team for the 1987 season. But just three days into spring training, it became clear that the popular manager, who had accumulated 404 wins during his 6-year tenure with the team, no longer had the stamina to continue. So he resigned, passing the reins to Billy Gardner, who led the team

to a second-place finish in the AL West in 1987. Unfortunately, Howser didn't live to see the end of that season. On June 17, at the age of 51, Howser passed away. On July 3, his uniform number (10) became the first number retired in Royals history, and Howser was inducted into the team's Hall of Fame. By the end of the year, the Dick Howser Trophy, college baseball's equivalent to football's Heisman Trophy, had been established, and Howser's alma mater, Florida State University, had renamed its field in honor of his contributions to their baseball program.

KEVIN APPIER

young pitcher Kevin Appier tallied 13 wins in 1991, while closer Jeff Montgomery earned 33 saves with an arsenal of pitches that included a devastating slider. "We called it the 'manhole slider,'" Royals pitcher Mike Boddicker said. "He threw it up there, and it disappeared down a manhole." Still, the 1991 Royals barely topped .500, going a mediocre 82–80.

THE DROUGHT BEGINS

n September 30, 1992, George Brett became only the 22nd player in history to join the 3,000-hits club. But after two decades in the game, his offensive production was starting to wane. In 1993, as his team put together an 84–78 record, the future Hall-of-Famer announced that he would be retiring from baseball. "I could have played another year, but I would have been playing for the money," Brett said. "Baseball deserves better than that."

Through their first 25 seasons, the Royals had won 6 division titles and 1 World Series. But by the mid-1990s, the small-market team was suddenly struggling to hold on to talented young players and remain competitive. Standout hurler David Cone did his best to help, winning 16 games in 1994. But in early August, with Kansas City at 64–51 and in third place in the new AL Central Division, a players' strike canceled the remainder of the season.

When the players returned in April 1995, Cone was gone. In his stead, Appier and Montgomery anchored the pitching staff. First baseman Wally Joyner and third baseman Gary Gaetti led the offense and helped the team go 70–74, good for second in the AL Central. A second-place finish was out of the question in 1996, though. For the first time in the team's 28-year history, Kansas City finished dead last in its division at 75–86, a full 24 games out of first place. In 1997, the Royals finished last again. In 1998, with the help of speedy outfielder Johnny Damon, who paced the team with 104 runs, the Royals barely escaped the cellar with a lowly 72–89 mark.

The Royals continued to lose at a rapid pace in 1999. The main bright spot of the season was Carlos Beltran, a first-year center fielder who belted 22 home runs and drove in 108 runs to win AL

CENTER FIELDER · AMOS OTIS

For 14 years, one of the most popular chants heard in Royals Stadium was "A-O, A-O," which heralded one of Amos Otis's dazzling plays in the outfield or his appearance at the plate. Although Otis was sometimes criticized for what appeared to be a lackadaisical attitude in the outfield, he was an excellent fielder who made difficult plays appear simple, making slick one-handed catches and smooth throws to the infield. He also hustled on the base paths, stealing 5 bases in one game and leading the league with 52 steals in 1971. Otis retired a year after leaving the Royals.

AMOS OTIS
CENTER FIELDER

KANSAS CITY
ROYALS

STATS

Royals seasons: 1970–83

Height: 5-foot-11

Weight: 166

- **5-time All-Star**

- **3-time Gold Glove winner**

- **193 career HR**

- **2,020 career hits**

Rookie of the Year honors. Royals fans also had the privilege that year of seeing one of their own ushered into baseball immortality, as George Brett was voted into the Baseball Hall of Fame in his first year of eligibility. "It's very, very special," Brett said at a news conference following the announcement. "When you start playing, it's a dream that you will make it, but you don't really think that dream will ever come true."

Even more disappointing than Kansas City's string of losing seasons in the late '90s were the team's continued financial problems. After the 2000 season, the cash-strapped Royals were forced to trade away both Damon and Jermaine Dye, a Gold Glove-winning outfielder who had led the team in home runs in 1999 and 2000. Still, team management attempted to stay upbeat. "We have the makings of a pretty good pitching staff in the works," said general manager Allard Baird. "Do we have some holes to fill? Yes, we do. But the bottom line is we're looking up in the standings, and we need to become a better ballclub."

NEW NOBLES

That better ballclub would take time to build. First baseman Mike Sweeney was consistently solid at the plate, third baseman Joe Randa showed a strong swing, and Beltran had developed into a legitimate power hitter, but the rest of the team struggled. The Royals' 2002 season ended in the club's first-ever 100-loss campaign.

After such a disappointing year, no one had high hopes for the 2003 Royals. But under new manager Tony Peña, the team won its first nine

KANSAS CITY'S CASTLE

The Kansas City Royals play their home games in one of the most beautiful parks in baseball—but Kauffman Stadium certainly isn't the newest. When it opened on April 10, 1973, Royals Stadium (as it was known until being renamed for owner Ewing Kauffman in 1993) was a state-of-the-art facility. It had artificial turf, distant outfield walls, and fountains just beyond the fences—a nod to Kansas City's reputation as "The City of Fountains." In the past two decades, the venue has been significantly renovated and modernized. In 1990, a JumboTron display board went up in left field, topped by the four golden prongs of the Royals' crown. In 1995, the turf, which had previously been considered a home advantage for the Royals, was replaced with natural grass, and its fountains were replaced by a "water spectacular," a grand, 322-foot-wide fountain that stretches into the left-field corner. Before the 2004 season began, the outfield walls were pushed back to their original dimensions of 330 feet in left and right fields, 410 in center, and 385 in both left-center and right-center, and in 2009, further renovations were made, including new scoreboards, reduced seating capacity, and improved concourses.

RIGHT FIELDER · BO JACKSON

Bo Jackson had two choices when he finished college in 1985: play pro football for the Tampa Bay Buccaneers or play baseball for the Kansas City Royals. He chose the Royals. But in 1987, his love of football prompted Jackson to announce that he would play for the Los Angeles Raiders as a "hobby" during baseball's off-season. Although Royals management wasn't happy, Jackson returned in 1988 to hit 25 homers—some of them monstrous blasts—and steal 27 bases. His two-sport career ended when he injured a hip playing football in 1990. He hit another 30 homers in parts of 3 seasons with 2 other teams before retiring in 1994.

STATS

Royals seasons: 1986–90

Height: 6-foot-1

Weight: 225

- **1989 All-Star Game MVP**

- **141 career HR**

- **415 career RBI**

- **82 career stolen bases**

BO JACKSON
RIGHT FIELDER

KANSAS CITY
ROYALS

MANAGER · DICK HOWSER

As a player, Dick Howser was a shortstop best known for his quick feet and solid swing. As a manager, he was recognized as the man who took over the Kansas City Royals in the midst of a strike-shortened 1981 season and, in four short years, turned them into world champions. While Howser was managing the AL All-Star team in 1986, broadcasters noticed him mixing up signals when he changed pitchers; two days later, he was diagnosed with a brain tumor. Howser tried to return to the dugout for the 1987 season but was too ill. He passed away 3 months later at the age of 51.

STATS

Royals seasons as manager: 1981–86

Managerial record: 507–425

World Series championship: 1985

DICK HOWSER
MANAGER

KANSAS CITY
ROYALS

games and ended April a remarkable 17–7. Even though injuries slowed the team's hot pace by midseason, the incredible offensive output of rookie shortstop Angel Berroa helped the Royals stay in contention through September. Although Kansas City ultimately fell short of the playoffs, the club took home lofty accolades when Berroa earned the Rookie of the Year award and Peña was honored as AL Manager of the Year.

On opening day of the 2004 season, the third-largest crowd in the history of Kauffman Stadium (formerly Royals Stadium) watched as Beltran hit a walk-off home run to seal a victory over the Chicago White Sox. Unfortunately, subsequent wins were few and far between. Beltran was traded away in June, and besides a franchise-record-setting 26–5 victory over the Detroit Tigers in September, there were few memorable moments. The Royals' 58–104 record set a new team record for most losses; in all of baseball, only the Arizona Diamondbacks, who finished 51–111, had a worse season.

The next three seasons weren't much better, as the Royals finished dead last in the AL Central each year. But a new crop of young players was showing signs of maturity. Right-handed pitcher Zack Greinke took most of the 2006 season off while dealing with an anxiety disorder, but he came back throwing heat that suggested he'd soon be living up to the potential that had made him a first-round pick in baseball's 2002 amateur draft. Solid third baseman Mark Teahen, slugging first baseman Billy Butler, and fleet-footed outfielder David DeJesus also looked impressive at times.

The first real signs of a turnaround occurred near the end of the 2008 season. New manager Trey Hillman had taken over full-time, and the players seemed to respond by getting stronger as the season progressed. In September, Kansas City went 18–8, and the Royals faithful started buzzing as the team finished out of the AL Central cellar for the first time in five seasons with a 75–87 record.

The Royals hoped to continue their ascent in 2009, and the new season started with a bang. Greinke was nearly unhittable in his first handful of starts as the Royals sprinted out to an 18–11 mark and a three-game lead in the AL Central in early May. After that, though, the offense labored to score runs, and a swoon dropped Kansas City back into last place again.

That season was not without bright spots, though. Second baseman Alberto Callaspo batted an even .300—his second straight season at or

A ROYAL MESS

By 2005, things had been going south for the Royals for more than a decade. The team hadn't had a winning season since 1993, and it had had to trade or give up many of its best players because of increasing salary demands. In 2003, though, the club pulled off a rather shocking 83–79 record. Hopes were high for similar success in 2004, but the Royals ended up sinking to a new low. They won only 7 games in all of April; by the end of May, they had added only 10 more. To make matters worse, it was clear that management was shopping young star Carlos Beltran around the league, hoping to trade the talented outfielder before losing him to free agency in the off-season. On June 24, Beltran was sent to the Houston Astros for two players and cash. The Royals responded by losing 14 of their next 16 games. In July, they suffered through an eight-game losing streak, then wrapped up September and started October by dropping another seven in a row. By the time the season mercifully ended on October 3, the Royals had set a franchise record for the most losses in a season, with 104.

DAVID DeJESUS

Energetic outfielder David DeJesus did his best to boost the struggling Royals, scoring an average of 93 runs a season from 2003 through 2010.

After the departure of star Zack Greinke (below) in late 2010, Joakim Soria (opposite) assumed the role of Kansas City's top gun on the pitching mound.

ZACK GREINKE

JOAKIM SORIA

above the .300 mark—and young, fireballing relief pitcher Joakim Soria notched 30 saves. Greinke, though, was the real talk of Kansas City, as he kept up his dominant pitching all season long and finished with a 16–8 record and a league-leading 2.16 earned run average (ERA)—accomplishments that earned him the Cy Young Award. Unfortunately, after the Royals ended up at the bottom of the division again in 2010, they traded the ace to the Milwaukee Brewers for four young players, including outfielder Lorenzo Cain. The loss of Greinke was painful, but Royals general manager Dayton Moore promised to rebuild around Butler and Soria. "We expect to be competitive next year," Moore said. "We're still working to improve our baseball team."

Kansas City has witnessed some phenomenal baseball since the Royals were born in 1969, including several epic postseason battles, one world championship, and legendary players with such names as Brett, Saberhagen, and White. Although times have been tough for Kansas City fans in recent years, the day may soon come when the Royals seize the crown as kings of baseball once again.

INDEX

Aikens, Willie 19

Appier, Kevin 33, 34

Baird, Allard 36

Baseball Hall of Fame 23, 33, 36

batting championships 10, 16, 30

Beltran, Carlos 34, 36, 37, 41, 43

Berroa, Angel 41

Boddicker, Mike 33

Brett, George 10, 15, 16, 19, 20, 23, 33, 36, 47

Butler, Billy 42, 47

Cain, Lorenzo 47

Callaspo, Alberto 42, 47

Cone, David 34

Cy Young Award 8, 25, 47

Damon, Johnny 34, 36

DeJesus, David 42

division championships 10, 15, 22, 33

Drago, Dick 9

Dye, Jermaine 36

Frey, Jim 15, 19

Gaetti, Gary 34

Gardner, Billy 31

Gold Glove award 18, 30, 35, 36

Greinke, Zack 41–42

Gubicza, Mark 25

Herzog, Whitey 15

Hillman, Trey 42

Howser, Dick 19, 26, 29, 31, 40

Jackson, Bo 29, 39

Joyner, Wally 34

Kansas City Athletics 6

Kansas City Monarchs 6, 12

Kauffman, Ewing 38

Kauffman Stadium 38, 41

Lemon, Bob 9

Manager of the Year award 41

McRae, Hal 19

Montgomery, Jeff 33, 34

Moore, Dayton 47

Municipal Stadium 9, 10

MVP award 8, 16, 26

Negro Leagues 6, 12

Orta, Jorge 24, 26

Otis, Amos 10, 35

Patek, Freddie 10, 28

Peña, Tony 37, 41

Piniella, Lou 9

playoffs 10, 15, 16, 19, 22, 25

  AL Championship Series 10, 15, 16, 19, 25

  AL Division Series 19

Porter, Darrell 13

Quisenberry, Dan 16, 19, 22

Randa, Joe 37

retired numbers 18, 31

Rojas, Cookie 10, 18

Rookie of the Year award 9, 36, 41

Royals Stadium 10, 38, 41

Saberhagen, Bret 8, 22, 25, 26, 47

Soria, Joakim 47

Sweeney, Mike 14, 37

Teahen, Mark 42

team records 10, 41, 43

White, Frank 15, 18, 47

Wilson, Willie 15–16, 19, 30

world championships 8, 24, 26, 33, 40, 47

World Series 8, 19, 24, 25, 26, 33